Sound Sense

A. E. TANSLEY, B.Sc., M.Ed.

BOOK 2

Illustrated by Jo Chesterman

Nelson

Here is a tree

Look at the picture. Say the word tree.
What sound does it end with?

Here are some more words with the ee
sound in them. See if you can read them:
   see bee need deep feed sweet
They all have the ee sound in them.
They all belong to the ee family.

2

EXERCISE 1

Find the <u>ee</u> family words. Write them in your book.

1   see week feet fed need
2   deep seem keep sheep red
3   heed miss seed sweet bee
4   feel seen feed fell been
5   they sleep seem this keep

EXERCISE 2

Draw your own picture of some sheep under a tree.

EXERCISE 3

Write these sentences in your book putting in the missing letters.

1   Wool comes from sh – – p.
2   I sl – – p in a bed.
3   I have two f – –t.
4   There are seven days in a w – –k.
5   Please k – – p off the grass.
6   Flowers grow from s – – ds.
7   John's mother gave him some sw – – ts.
8   Mary f – – ds her dog every day.
9   The water was very d – – p.
10 On Saturday I m – – t my pal.
11 I can s – – the b – – on that flower.

12 I have a sh − − t on my bed.
13 My pen has a st − − l nib.
14 Yesterday I did not f − − l very well.
15 There are a lot of w − − ds in our garden.

EXERCISE 4

Here is a word but the letters are in the wrong order — rete. When we put the letters in the right order we get the word tree.

Now here are some more words with the letters in the wrong order: dees, weke, twese, eeb, tefe.

Put the letters in the right order then write a sentence for each of the words.

Look at the m<u>oo</u>n

Look at the picture. Say the word m<u>oo</u>n. What sound does <u>oo</u> make? Here are some more words with the <u>oo</u> sound in them. See if you can read them:

   t<u>oo</u> c<u>oo</u>l f<u>oo</u>d n<u>oo</u>n r<u>oo</u>f c<u>oo</u>p

   s<u>oo</u>n sch<u>oo</u>l r<u>oo</u>m f<u>oo</u>l

EXERCISE 5

Find the <u>oo</u> family words. Write them in your book.

1   noon soon feed roof week sleep
2   tree cool room here they school
3   food cap can fool too seem
4   feeding fooling feeling cooling selling
5   schools sheep lips fools tells room

EXERCISE 6

Draw a picture of your school.

EXERCISE 7

Write these sentences in your book putting in the missing letters.

1   The m − − n was in the sky.
2   The house had a green r − − f.
3   The r − − m was full of people.
4   Do not play the f − − l at sch − − l.
5   It will s − − n be time to go home.
6   We need f − − d to keep us fit.
7   We keep our b − − ks in the classr − − m.
8   We sleep in a bedr − − m.

EXERCISE 8

Here is a word but the letters are in the wrong order – omon. When we put the letters in the right order we get the word moon.

Now here are some more words with the letters in the wrong order: moro, loof, foro, hoolsc, doof.
Write a sentence for each of the words.

EXERCISE 9

1   Look at these words.
    here bee her moon sat the there
    tell shoot cool and seen
Write in your book the ones you can make from school-teacher.

2   Look at these words.
    ball mat hill poor bell roof fat
    root and at bat fell
Write in your book the words you can make out of football-player.

3   Now see how many words you can make out of television-room and write them in your book.

EXERCISE 10

More than one.

1   We say one room but two _____ .
2   We say one _____ but four schools.
3   We say one _____ but many seeds.
4   We say one football but six _____ .
5   We say one cup but several _____ .
6   We say one sheep and many _____ .
7   We say one _____ but four weeks.
8   We say one sweet but a bag of
    _____ .

9 We say one house but several _____ .
10 We say one _____ but two apples.

EXERCISE 11

Find the word in the box which belongs to the same family. Write the family in your book.

1 see deep keep

2 cool soon too

3 meet seem week

| egg wet feet |
| box room doll |
| bee ten met |

4	noon food roof	hot not moon
5	bit fit tin	his too let
6	sell well fell	rat tell tree
7	gas sad man	said can this
8	fun nut cup	bell hug pen
9	pot not got	boy girl lot
10	needs keeps seems	full feels up

EXERCISE 12

Put these words into families.

1   cool soon need see too bee feet roof
2   week moon been tree noon meet food
    school
3   leg hot fell men on got met dog
4   had tub fun an hug gas sad full

Now find three more words for these families.

5   feel seed been _____ _____ _____
6   fill miss hill _____ _____ _____
7   bed let men _____ _____ _____
8   room roof soon _____ _____ _____

EXERCISE 13

Find the stranger in these families.

1 box lip lot dog on God got off
2 hat man see cap am fat bag can
3 big feet mill fill kiss hill miss bill
4 moon school fell room too cool
5 meeting needing cooling feeling seeing keeping
6 fun cup but seed tub us gun
7 pen red moon ten fed wet men
8 feel seen deep week feet room tree
9 food noon sheep too fool roof soon
10 bee keep need sweet seem school been

EXERCISE 14

Write these sentences in your book putting in the missing letters.

1 I go to sch – – l every day.

12

2   I like sw — — ts.
3   There is a tr — — in the garden.
4   I saw the man in the m — — n.
5   Sheep f — — d on grass.
6   Are you f — — ling well?
7   Can you s — — me?
8   The school has a red r — — f.

EXERCISE 15

Write each set of words in your book. Now join with a line the words that go together. The first one is done for you.

1   fit   killing
    kill   fitting
    filling — fill

2   greet   get
    getting   greeting
    cut   cutting

3   missing kissing
    kiss   boxing
    box   miss

4   see   needing
    meet   seeing
    need   meeting

5   kill   kiss
    cutting   killing
    kissing   cut

6   sleeping   feeding
    feed   feeling
    feel   sleep

EXERCISE 16

Write each set of words in your book. Now join with a line words beginning with the same letter. The first one is done for you.

1   bee   roof
    room   noon
    need   been

2   here   first
    fun   has
    ten   top

3   feet   wet
    week   sad
    seed   food

4   let   little
    kill   pet
    pot   keep

5   boot   deep
    get   bad
    did   got

6   cool   too
    tree   seen
    soon   can

Find five words beginning with the same letter as <u>been</u>. Write them in your book.

Find five words beginning with the same letter as <u>sell</u>. Write them in your book.

Choose the right word and write the sentence in your book.

1   I am (seed, sleep, meeting) my father.

2   I have two (soon, school, feet).
3   The (bell, bed, moon) is in the sky.
4   The water was (keep, deep, week).
5   There is a (see, bee, been) on the flower.
6   I have (seen, been, need) on my holidays.
7   It will (soon, moon, seen) be time for school.
8   Peter went to (school, sheep, sleep) on a (bed, bad, mill).
9   A (sleep, sheep, football) has four (feel, moon, feet).

EXERCISE 18

Put the words in these sentences in the right order.

1   dog. I have a
2   two I feet. have
3   feeling am I ill.
4   meeting I father. my am
5   like to school. I going
6   trees. Apples on grow
7   football We school. at play
8   always sweet. is Sugar
9   sky. The moon in the is
10 car ran the man over. The

EXERCISE 19

Here are some sentences. Read each one carefully. If you think it makes sense put "This is right." If you think it is silly put "This is wrong."

1   My mother is two years old.
2   There are seven days in every week.
3   We have our food on the roof.

4   There are trees in a wood.
5   I have seen a boy playing football.
6   A bee can sting you.
7   Trees have no roots.
8   The sky is in the moon.
9   Sheep have six legs.
10 A dog can run.

EXERCISE 20

Put these words in families and write them in your book. There are four words for each family.

moon at feed cup hug hot food
eggs off sheep bad kill am met
cap soon leg bed cut steep meeting
on but his root miss not lips

Here is a story for you to read.

A DAY OFF SCHOOL

It was Saturday and John Smith had the day off school. His mother let him stay in bed but he could not sleep. He soon got up and had a hot cup of tea and an egg for his breakfast.

As he was having his breakfast the bell rang. Mother went to the door. It was John's pal Dick. "Can John come out to play football?" said Dick. John's mother said, "He can come out to play but he must not play football. He has cut his leg." When John had finished his breakfast he and Dick went out to play.

EXERCISE 21

Now you have read the story answer these questions.

1   What is the name of the story?
2   What did John have for his breakfast?
3   What day was it?
4   Who rang the bell?
5   Why did John's mother say he could not play football?
6   How many people are there in the story?
7   Who had the day off school?
8   Why didn't John stay in bed?
9   Who went to answer the door?
10 What would you like to do if you had the day off school?

EXERCISE 22

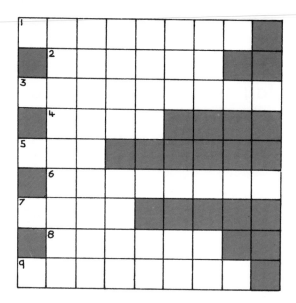

Make a copy of this word puzzle then put the right words in the right places. All the words are in the story you have just read.

1   What day was it?
2   Who let John stay in bed?
3   John had an egg for his _____ .
4   Who rang the bell?
5   John had cut his _____ .
6   Dick wanted John to play at _____ .
7   John could not _____ football.
8   John had a day off _____ .
9   John had _____ his breakfast.

EXERCISE 23

Choose the right word and write the sentence in your book.

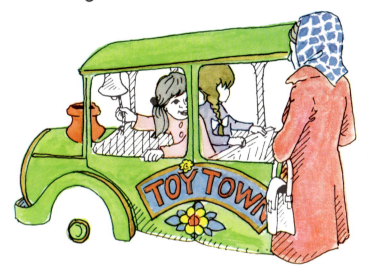

1 I _____ the bell. (ring, sing, fill)
2 The box was made of _____ . (wool, wood, went)
3 The hill was _____ . (steep, stool, school)
4 Sheep _____ on grass. (feet, feed, feel)
5 I _____ in a bed. (steep, sleep, sheep)
6 The stool _____ four legs. (his, him, has)
7 The cup was _____ of water. (fill, full, feed)
8 I saw some _____ . (man, can, men)

9 I ate _____ apple. (an, a, am)
10 The _____ boy _____ the girl.
    (bad, bit, bag) (hit, fit, sit)

EXERCISE 24

Here are some puzzles for you to do.
The answers are in the wrong places.
Write down the number of the puzzle in
your book and put the right answer at the
side.

1   We see it at night.   cut
2   A game for boys.   week
3   We eat this.   moon
4   To stand on.   see
5   To drink from.   egg
6   This bleeds.   stool
7   For shopping.   feet
8   Seven days.   football
9   We do this with our eyes.   cup
10 To sit on.   bag

EXERCISE 25

Here is a story that is mixed up. Write it out so that it makes sense.

MY BIRTHDAY

I will give all my friends a piece of cake.
On Saturday it is my birthday.
I will cut the cake at my party.
Mother has made a cake for me.
I will be nine years old.
I am going to have a party.

Here is a story for you to read.

MARY'S DOG

Mary has a dog. His name is Rick. She had him for her birthday. At night he sleeps in a bed made out of a big box. As soon as Mary comes home from school she takes Rick out. She has to keep him on a lead. One day he bit a man. The man had to go to hospital. A policeman came to Mary's house. He told Mary she would get into trouble if Rick bit anyone again.

EXERCISE 26

Now you have read the story answer these questions.

1 Who has a dog?
2 What is the name of the dog?
3 Where does it sleep?
4 When does Mary take the dog out?
5 What did the dog do?
6 Where did the man have to go?
7 Who came to Mary's house?
8 What will happen if the dog bites anyone again?

EXERCISE 27

Make a copy of this word puzzle in your book. See if you can put the right words in the right places. All the words you will need are in the story you have just read.

1 Mary's dog was named _____.
2 She got the dog for her _____.
3 The dog sleeps in a _____.
4 Mary keeps her dog on a _____.
5 The dog _____ a man.
6 They had to take the man to _____.
7 A policeman came to Mary's _____.
8 Rick must not bite anyone _____.

28

EXERCISE 28

Put the words in these sentences in the right order.

1 feel did well. She not
2 her Mother to bed. told to go
3 did She some reading.
4 home. her sent teacher The
5 to went Mary school.

Now put the sentences in order.

EXERCISE 29

Here are some sentences. Read each one carefully. If you think it makes sense put "This is right." If you think it is silly put "This is wrong."

1 We see with our eyes.
2 A house has a roof.
3 A bad man is good.
4 A box is made of wool.
5 I go to school to sleep.
6 The moon is full of cheese.
7 I use my feet for football.
8 Sheep feed on grass.

Here is a story for you to read.

CROSSING THE ROAD

John was eleven years old. He had a friend named Peter. They both went to the same school. On the way to school they had to cross a busy street. One day they forgot what they had to do before they crossed the street. A big car hit them but they were not hurt. The car pulled up in time.

Now when John and Peter have to cross a busy street they look right, then they look left, then they look right again. If it is safe they cross.

EXERCISE 30

Now you have read the story answer these questions.

1   What was the name of John's friend?
2   What did John and Peter have to do on the way to school?
3   Why were John and Peter hit by the car?
4   What would you do before you crossed a busy street?
5   How old was John?

Draw a picture of John and Peter.

EXERCISE 31

Here is a story that is mixed up. Write it out so that it makes sense.

AN ACCIDENT

She was in hospital for a long time.
A policeman sent for a car.
An old lady was crossing the street.
Now she is better and has gone home.
The car took her to the hospital.
A lorry ran over her.

EXERCISE 32

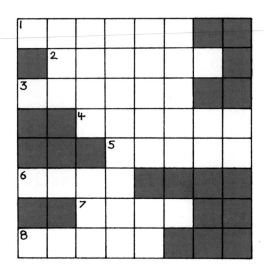

Make a copy of this word puzzle then put the right words in the right places. All the words are in the story you have just read on page 30.

1 How old was John?
2 John and Peter had to cross a _____ .
3 They _____ what they had to do.
4 The car _____ up in time.
5 Now they look _____ .
6 Then they look _____ .
7 Then they _____ right again.
8 If it is safe they _____ the street.

EXERCISE 33
Now write a story about an accident.